TABLE

M000313714

5
UN-RISEN WORDS

Christmas Sting
Endless Life
Released Thoughts
Bittersweet I Sleep
Happiness
I Matter
Alone Journey
Sleep Creeps
Me
Passionate Thoughts
Bubble Me Up
Drifting Sea
Scripted Life
Unspoken Life
Bitter Life
A Journey Life
The Past Me
Dreaded Soul
Blue Life
Unreasonable I See
Dong
Swish Wash
Unnamed Return
Yes, Indeed
Double Lines
Precious Memories
Clouds
Hurting Mind
Challenged Life
Free at Last
Dream On, Dream On
Wondering Life
Ridden Beyond Belief
Floating Raft
Disguise Fly
My Last Breath
Road to Despair
Underneath the Tree
A Sinner's Soul
Sneeze Breeze Delight
He's Been Away

Silent Conversation
Good Side in Me
Funny Life

6
DRIFTED WINDS

Hanging from a Tree
Twisted Mind Set Free
Finally Set Free
My Past Is Gone
Past, You Must Go
Since I Meet You
Weary Soul
Eyes of Misery
Trodden Despair
Devil's Defeat
I Trust Me and Not You
Whisper Surprise
Forgotten
Me Be Me
Redeemed and Set Free
Drywalls Victory
Bare Feet and Pregnant
Dream On
Unconscious Worry
Worry Swell
Happy Glee
Silent Voice
Hidden Me
Disappointed Hope

7
MISSISSIPPI

Mississippi Grounds
My Mississippi Music
My Mississippi
Mississippi Sing On
Mississippi River's Path
Mississippi Blues
Howlin' Wolf Ground
March On, My Brother, My Friend, My Sister, My People

Rhythm Cool Blues
B. B. King String
Magnolia Tree
Mississippi
He Found Me Again

Art Despair by Visual Artist Linda Kay Chandler

AUTHOR'S PREFACE

The author captured the front and back cover picture of the sun. This collection of poetry has been part of my life. I have always written things down that God has spoken to me over the years. Awaken early one morning; the Holy Father revealed to me my poetry in a poetry collection that will be partof my writing ministry. God has used me as His vessel in the gift of working many miracle, and prophecies over the years. I'll discuss some of the miracle and prophecies in my upcoming book. "Preach, and you teach the Word, and you will blossom beautifully like your Pear Trees outside," was the command spoken by God in 2009. Years prior, I had been doing this unaware of my calling. Now, I had a holy calling on my life to have compassion for God's chosen people, help heal their lives, help them discover the best in themselves, and help lead them to their purpose and mission in life so that they may prosper. As a young child, I was bold and tenacious; I held a tight hold to my dreams while looking up into the clouds one day, I said, "I will attend a major university, I will be an author, and all my dreams will come true." The children and adults chuckled at my words. I started writing to become an author when I was directed to my elementary school library by my teacher. As I approached the library, I was overwhelmed at all the books that were in there. I said, "I am going to read all of them." Every day I would check out several books. One day the Librarian said, "You will be an author one day." I smiled and said, "Yes, I will." I read every book in that library and left proof by making sure that I signed each book. Years later, I was at a PTA meeting, and they were giving away the library books. My nieces and nephews came up to me and said, "Auntie Linda, your name is in all of these books." I said, "Yes, they are." I was so happy that I had left my signature in all those books. I worked hard to obtained my High School Equivalency Diploma, earned my

Associate degree in Microcomputer Technology, a Bachelor of Science in Interdisciplinary Studies with emphasis in General Business, Business Technology, and Apparels Textiles & Merchandising, and pursued my Master of Public Policy & Administration degree all while taken care of my special needs child and battling many trials, tribulations, and triumphs as a divorcee of three children. My tuition was paid off in full. I am a work in progress. This book was inspired by my daughter Epilepsy Journey. The Glory goes to God.

My world is spiritual because of God.

1
PRESIDENTS' POEMS

Donald and Melania Trump
Make America Great Again

A land that is strong, free, and powerful.
We stand united in unity and strength as a torch to light up the world for
what will stand. We put our citizens first to Make America Great Again.
Work needs to be done as a country to renew its strength. America will lead
the country, and it will not be a glance. As our country, brave warriors lead
our country not to be at ease to secure our veterans on hand.
A beautiful land so richly deserves the best as infrastructure upgrades in our
nation's land. Not neglecting the drug epidemic that will eventually stop as
we look forward to beautifying our entire cities as I keep my promise to
Make America Great Again.

I received a letter from former President Donald J. Trump.

Michelle and Obama
Goodbye

I'm with her, and she is with me.
I will buy her ice cream when she doesn't want pie.
Together in history, we've made a change for all to see,
while questioning my citizen and faith in reality.
To make a better place for you and me because of my character and
conviction for good, hardworking people like you and me.
We have worked together to change the lives of people in every word and
action that matters responsibly.
Springing the love from our hearts, we have for our children that inspire
your children and us across the country to let move and be happy to know
that everyone matters.
We work to make a difference for our children and yours not to go low, but
high.
We emphasize the hard drive to continue promoting a change not just for
now, but for the world to come as champions because we are stronger
together in a great country.
We continue to linger on to the end of what's to come.
We hope that our legacy will continue to change lives to come in who you
are and what you can be as we leave something better for you to come.
On a day when the calm wind breezes a stroke of enlightenment about the
choices to come, linger on as we both speak that freedom will soon come,
as we continue to fight to give a chance for everyone to succeed.
And not be a moment late when our purpose for our journey has spurned for
ourselves and to our family.
We see a glimpse of what it will be as we hope not in disparity, but a glee of
a sigh of relief as this country moves forward as a village with you and me.
All have come and will continue to fall in a sigh as we move about in the
White House. The night air engulfs the memories of pleasant dreams as we
say goodbye.

I received a letter from former President Barack Obama and
first Lady Michelle Obama.

I Didn't Think I Mattered

On the verge of quitting
I poured everything into what mattered.
But still, I didn't think that I matter the most.
The fear of crippling thoughts
that I wasn't validated seemed so far away
until a chance encounter of words
that I frequently spoke to my students that each of you matter.
Inspiring to say you are valuable,
but now I know today
that I am valued the most
when *I didn't think that I mattered* today.

Publication in The Starkville Daily News
Inspired from my daughter Precious Nicole Epilepsy Journey

QUOTES by Linda Kay Chandler

Life sharpens us to be wise if we accept it.

Dream big to think big. Be inspired to encourage someone else because love is the greatest gift of all.

Uncertainty is genuine if all you have in life is nothing to do.

I must be proud of what I am trying to do. I must never let it lose its ground.

Uphold my beauty; it's all I have as I am being engulfed by love of a pleasant sound.

2
WONDERING THOUGHTS

POEM
Oprah Winfrey
OWN
by
Mississippi Poet
Linda Kay Chandler

Poem Oprah Winfrey
OWN

A world chosen for me despite how I came to be,
gifted as a child that only I could see my life in front of me.
At what lies ahead of me because of my chosen destiny.
The roots of my grandmother's upbringing set my faith on the path.
I would be as I am surrounded by what lies ahead of me.
That will try to overtake and to engulf me to neglect me.
But my father wouldn't let that happen to me.
I am setting my strong working ethics on a path where I needed to be.

As I walk the straight line ahead of me,
headed toward my destiny.
Compassion overwhelms me as I give to give
so much more than what people can see
while giving engulfs me to prune me.
My calling, I now see the real soul within me.
A mother's love for those that allures me
to spring them forth into what they need to be.
I see the love for my girls because they are me;
my heart for my sweet dogs that only speak
in sounds that only I behold to believe.
As I read to see the other side in people, that's told.
Enlightenment touches my soul
while calling my soul to be its own.

Poem Oprah Winfrey Giver

She has the heart of a joyous giver.
She gives love to even the deceiver.
She touches the hearts of many giving.
She is hoping that all would be touched and be a giver,
while knowing and finding their way.
And bringing God's life to all someday
as I am Oprah Winfrey, the giver.

I Will Rise Up

Arise to a new territory and seek your determined destination.
Rise again to stand where you belong to meet your purpose and
greet your destiny.
Rise to see your dreams unfold as you wonder and behold.

That I will take you to new level that meet your goals.
Rise to take back all that you held.
Even that I cannot see for me because I am valuable enough to
destroy my enemy.
I will rise, and this time, I can't destroy me because I entitled to be.
My dreams have risen.
My purpose has risen.
My destiny has risen.
My goals have risen.
My request is known.
I have risen to stand and be true to myself because of my integrity values
who I am, what I'm created to be.

Matter

A journey of discipline is the quest of that journey to know why it exists.
The mission of the unknown lingers by briefly only to see the existence of
time and present while others linger on in prosperity. The journey of life
is strange to the eye of reality. When we investigate the unknown things of
this world, one must adventure at a sideway of time and presence
to know how it will stop that time.
Linger on into the existence of time to breathe its atmosphere of life to bare
time. See if those that must be as they were not confused with that time of
space when it matters the most.
Infrequent of time must be mapped out with time to know the existence of
that time and question when it matters the most. How is the indifference of
time different than that time that matters the most?
All will know the one who brings new life into the *matter* when it matters
the most. Yes, it must *matter* when you speak things into existence while
helping those who need it the most and never forget the lost stolen in the
soul. While life brings the pleasure of time, sometimes it brings experience
when it matters the most.
You must remember how it begins for you when the time of issues of
existence lingers into space of time.
Not all will know when I speak a word into time, but you will know the
indifference of space and *matter* because it matters the most, especially
when you can't see or find it. I am dear to all who see me and know my
power of love. Wait for that new breath of life to breathe in the existence of
time and *matter* when it matters the most.

7

The indifferent in you must be in the presence of issues of the unknown truths of time.
I need more of you, but you need more of me simultaneously of existence.
All I'll need is you to be you when the time is right for the *matter* to *matter* the most.
Breathe and love to breathe the newness of this life when issues of being the most matter.
The indifference of time and space do *matter* when it's new.
Wait on the things of God, and it will be pleasant to your soul.
Now that time has lingered on in space, know now about how it matters only when that time must seek other time of space.
Time of existence waits for no one to be. And when that time speaks, all will know how that time and *matter* exists. Discipline the mind when the mind matters the most.
All will see that issues of time matters the most when you know that time is nearby you.
Wait not on the unknown to bring you nothing, but gather the hidden things to bring you the laughter of space and time.
Be active in all things, not in just what you want to be.

I Wrote You an Open Letter

I wrote you this letter.
And I hope it finds you. I hope it finds you.
My words will express how I feel about you.
I once was reminded inside how you once made me feel
when I think of you and the awful tears.
For you stole my innocence and my joy.
Now I am set free to love my life just as it should be.

True Love at Its Highest Peak

Was there truth between him and me?
I can't say it was love, but it must have been me.
Love comes and goes into the air.
What was I thinking to be open to these foes?
I was lusting after his spirit as if he was a legend of gold.
Hoping that he was the right one
who could rescue me from this life, you see?
Maybe it was lust.

Maybe it was me.
Maybe it seemed right to love you once.
You captured my heart when it was true,
while I was trying to find myself
from this glooming past of how I used to be.
Can I allow this to happen again?
Maybe this man is just for me.
I found it not to be.
I came cunning as a serpent
walking smoothly,
talking smoothly with sparkles in his eyes.
I clinched at that moment.
I discovered later he captured me with his deception.
I was hoping that he's finally the one.
Knowing within my heart
that *true love at its highest peak*
must be the right love to set me free.

A Survivor

A survivor of domestic violence.
Invaluable to him that abused me.
I grieved and devalued to the relationship
that kept me bound that entangled me.
Deceived by the conception, he came to steal, kill,
and destroy me.
The nurturer in me said, "He needs me."
My empathy and compassion help entrapped me not to be free.
Shameful to say, I am a person mentally, emotionally, physically, and
financially damaged. I was still bond to him
to heal him that deceived me
even though I needed healing myself.
As he said, "I will love you to death."
I knew that I had to escape so I would be free of this abuse.
Only a conversation with God saved me
to know that authentic love doesn't abuse me,
but honor, respect, and love didn't surround me.
Now I am set free from my misery to be worthy of love.
A survivor.
Who is a priceless, a beautiful gemstone, valuable, virtuous,

and, most of all, loved.

Wondrous Bridge

A *wondrous bridge* breathes new life, you see.
A life from the devil flees.
A fleet of hell he tried to entrap me to be.
But wait, I see another love moment from God.
That will protect me and set me free.

The First Child Speaks

Speaking with power and authority, only he can see
as others fringe with fear from his unknown words of the magi lac fear.
As he calmly says to himself, "I must speak."
Fringing from within, he says,
"I am the firstborn child. I must speak, you see."
The helpless feeling from within me won't let me be.
If I may speak, then one can see my pain, my infirmities,
and my past so I can set myself free
because I am the first child to speak.

The Still Voice

The still voice of a silent whisper stills the mind.
As it reaches us into a distant time,
reassuring us about the stillness of time.
As it leads you to find the new things in life,
on a journey, it finds to be kind.
Calming and comforting as we take another positive look at life.
Meditating and relaxing the mind, body, and soul.
I find it to be the true secret of God's heart
as *the still voice* speaks within the still mind.

Love the Life Your Living

Some people think they've gone as far as they can.
As they hope to regain life again,
While trying to figure out if life worth living, worth giving.

To love life worth living
as they live the life
to enjoy the life your living.

Fun Laughter

Laughter is fun
when you laugh so hard
hoping to forget what the past has done.
Maybe I'll laugh more
hoping this time
I can forget
just what *fun laughter* explores.

Supposed Life

Well maybe
I was just supposed to be me.
In this life
only God can see.
If I breakthrough
or will life break me?
Maybe one day
I'll see
where in life I'm supposed to be.

Catch of Breath

Catch a breath
and do not wonder
if life is for you
or maybe it's for me.
Someone else
to wonder,
how was a breath supposed to be?
The ear engulfs me.
With pain from my past
that won't let me be
as I breathe in and out, each breath has caught up with me.

11

The Will to Fight

The voice of a whisper cries
deep within my soul.
Trying to get through
and hoping for one's delight.
Enlarging me with a purpose.
Will I have *the will to fight?*

Pear Trees

The sun shines on my face.
As I look at the *pear trees*
blooming outside beneath me,
beaming against my cheek
as I was listening to the birds sing.
They take me into utter delight.
As the sun shines upon my face
to bring me a new light.

A Good Day

It's a beautiful day
as I am in my bed.
I am looking through my glass door
as God's sunbeams over my head.
It's going to be a beautiful day
because I can feel that it's going
to be *a good day.*
I know that today
will be even a better day.

Sneeze

Sneeze
in the breeze,
while I am in this hole
of unforgettable dreams.
I dream that one day it will come true.

And all I see is that to be *sneeze* breeze true.

Chuckling Birds

Birds are chuckling
and singing, I think.
As I wonder,
could they be secretly talking to me?
I wish I knew, I wish I knew
when I hear them singing?
Different sounds in harmony.
They must be praying
just like me.
Hoping that one day
we will all talk together
and walk together as the chuckling bird sings to me.

Eyes of a Child

Wisdom beholds the *eyes of a child*.
I am seeing and knowing their true destiny.
To live and let life live so the complications of the *eyes of a child* would
flee from me.

Protect Me, Lord

God will protect me
as I journey from place to place.
Underneath my feet,
God will capture me.
He won't let me fall
when I am faithful to Him.
He will protect me
even when I sleep.
I am driving on this dreary road.
God is here with me.
For me,
even when I can't sleep.
He is a true God

to all who care to protect them as they sleep.

Fullest Life

Live life to the fullest
with your all dreams insight so
you may not forget the whole experience in flight.

Never Give Up

I was tenacious and looked to the clouds,
speaking with authority
that all my dreams will come true.
Just as I see them to be,
because God never gave up on me.
He said, "*Never give up* on what I have for you
because someday you will be how I made you to be.
And that's true to be you."

Just for You

You breathe upon my neck.
You hold me in your arms.
You laugh with me.
You guided me with your soft gestures
that was *just for you.*

Oh, Just You

Oh, how can I be lost in the dawn of the night?
When your shadow breathes deeply upon me
like a high guiding light.
Just how you, my love.
Oh, just you.

A Life That Chooses Me

Away with the rules
that can sometimes be cruel.
On the life that chooses me, and I not thee.
Without my reasoning and permission
as if I gave into the fight.
To lose the battle
to be me
never to be seen or heard again
in *a life that chooses me.*

Youthfulness

Stricken from her youth,
her beauty on the outside
floated within her.
Her beautiful curly hair
taken from her youth.
As she smiled on the outside,
no one knew her pain inside.
Bruised and an enslaved by trade.
Her stricken hands bleed
from the curse of her flesh.
Pierce with holes upon her head
as she wondered. If I am a child.
Maybe I'm not. I am the child of the beholder
sent on a mission to show and give love
even to the undeserving.
Man, after women,
friend after friend,
family after man.
My Lord, when will my *youthfulness* begin?

Green Tree Drought

Well, another green tree has come and gone,
and now you're older.
Recapturing all that will behold your journey
as you gather the unknowns of the future forgotten drought
that will bring you joy if you don't get way into a life of *green tree drought.*

3
TRODDEN SACRIFICES

Guns and America

Anguish incident after incident that cries in no return
from gun made by Industrialists Samuel Colt and Oliver Winchester
as a tool to use as if it was for fun.
I lift my voice to take no sides.
Not to cast judgment, only to cast light.
It grows stronger and stronger about our Second Amendment Bill of Rights
from conversations of advocates on each side sincerely committed
to the Twenty-First Century debate of gun on the rise.
Are guns safe to be used for good people when so many innocent people are
murdered?
The nation's gun once breezed cool news.
Do we not carry our gun, only to be gunned down by someone who has lost
their way?
Only to think for a moment, I only want to be safe if I am in a gun battle
one day.
But what if my child is eager to play and accidentally pick up my gun
and shoot someone one day?

What if a mad person got a hold of a gun one day
only to kill all in the way. Would it be a way of life to keep our guns by our
sides to be safe out of harm's way?
I am trying to keep the next generation safe
before they are all killed off as if they are distinct prey.
Can we end gun violence in a nation with many guns?
That has become discomforted and distorted with the sight of so many guns.
Should we go back and look to enforce another Federal Gun Control
Legislation to reduce gun violence in a world that has lost its way?
Or should we hope that people would stop killing innocent people
like they murdered Dr. Martin Luther King, President John F. Kennedy,
and his brother without a cause?
History must be known for its mass shooting that seeks the souls of the
innocent carved in stones that will be forever before our eyes to wonder and
behold.

Distance Me

Why *distant me* when I am like you?
My skin,
my hair,
my body,
my organ,
all the same kind as you.
My pain goes deeper when my weight falls upon you.
Not to hate me but to understand that all I want is the same as you.
Love that
I seek to *distance me* from you.

Entangled Soul

The wondrous woes are gathering to entangle my soul.
I am trying to stay true to who I want to be.
But the pains of this world act as I am better than the rest.
How can you deny my freedom when God has chosen the best?
The best in me is who I can be.
People can see
that I am glorious in the state I am,

not ashamed to be different because I know where I stand.
Right side road so why entangle my spirit with hate
because it will not penetrate my soul.

Frowns

I know who I am.
Regardless of all those *frowns*
that is looking at me as if I am not free.
But wait and see who I am
because what I remember about Jesus
is that He died for me.

Can You Hear Me?

He is a person who loves I can't say.
Her tender touch is contrary and away.
Speaking with love, I still can't say.
She batters on about the children in such an awful away.
A person's love maybe one day.
Will I ever feel it on this here day?
Probably not until you can see
how important it is for me.
Distance in her thought because she has lost her way.
I hope she finds it today,
and not let love floats away.
As I speak, *can you hear me* today?

Mother's Day

Mothers, you are a priceless spirit
given as a vessel by Jehovah God that
reflects the unmeasurable real value of love.
How can I capture your unique power of fulfillment?
The creation of life you bring into this world.
Nurturing and loving are introduced only by you
and esteeming the highest honor that only a mother can give you.
Solely provided by God with honors for you on *Mother's Day*.

M - You meant the world.
O - On a journey that never could be.
T - Where I found you, a mystery could be true.
H - Oh How I journey on.
E - In an Everlasting world.
R - Running trying to find your
S - Sweetness.
D -The Day I realized how life would be without you.
A - Drifting away on a day, I could not say.
Y - But yonder, I found you deep within my soul as your love entrapped
me.

Fearless to Be

Will they forgive me for what I've done?
As a tough woman's love who guided their growth with love
and who guided their growth with fun,
I am ashamed of the unknown fears of what they will become.
Will I give them enough love so they will see?
I am a fearless woman who just wanted them to be free.

I Must Let Her Go

Tomorrow she must go.
Just for a little while, until I am healed and well.
To take on the world's care.
That is desperate to see.
I must let her go again.
She will progress and be free.
Into a young lady, she'll blossom to be.
That will know the way of life.
Into a world, she will soon be.
But the silence tears want, let me be.
Peace within me has lost its flight.
And I wonder if I will ever receive
her love for the last time tonight.

My Daughter's Voice

As I lie in my bed awake,
peace and love surround me.
I hear my daughter's beautiful voice say, "Mother."
But there's no one here but me.
Startled by her voice,
I sprang into action.
I am praying against the principality.
Then, peace and love surround me
to let me know that you're gifted to see and hear spiritually.
As I leaped up to call her
on the phone to say,
"Mommy loves you."
Now, I know that I heard *my daughter's voice*
in the spirit when all she wanted was to say,
"I hope to see you
another day."

Time Has Come

I've taken you this far,
as far as I can go.
Now it's time for me to let you go,
to be free in this world.
That may bring you grief and misery.
The *time has come.*
I must let you go.

Precious Is Her Name

Her mother said, "If I had a daughter.
I would name her Precious,
because she would be precious to me.
As she lingers upon my back to sleep,
Precious will be her name,
because it would be different for all to see."
That she will live up to her name
by proclaiming the right to her gain was
the name given to her by her mother

as she heard it in the night that
Precious is her name.

Take Care of Me

Take care of me because I was here for you.
When you were young, I took care of you.
One day I heard you say, "That's enough. Let me go."
Opportunities passed me by
because I wanted to raise you.
Now that you're gone, you have left me all alone
and forgot how I was faithful to you.
I wanted you to have a life that had passed me.
But I wanted better for you so
one day you would see that I left it all so you would *take care of me.*

Who Are You?

What kind of man is this?
Here he comes again
drunk and staggering.
I wonder about tonight.
Will we live in the pig's trout?
Will we have to run?
When we hear his shotgun?
Sometimes we would break
anything insight
as we are laughing at the sight
as this man would shoot with his shotgun
anything in sight.

Life

What does *life* mean?
All I can remember is the pain.
Wondering day after day,
would I live to see another day

as I regain my strength
so I might know what love is from a stranger?
Who speaks into my sleep?
Who has given me more love in my heart than I can keep?
Deep down within, I say what does life mean?
They only made me weak to be reliable, all alone in life.

We Didn't Know

We didn't know.
How a lady should
carry herself with dignity.
We didn't know
about the birds and bees
that would keep us free
from a life of misery.
We didn't know how to choose a man
that would be a plan.
To marry a good man. *We didn't know.*

A Sacrifice

I gave away my life
when you were young.
I gave away my career.
I did it all for you to one day obtain an education
and someday be all that you could be.
Washed away dreams and hope left me.
I realized that you would never be here for me.
Did I waste it all to be there for you?
I needed someone to help me to be me.
Should I've lived the life I wanted to be?
And now I genuinely say what about me?
I endured the past that passes me.
Was it worth *a sacrifice* of all that I lost for my life
and a career that left me?
I lost myself and you when I was only true,
when no one was there.
Now, you have lost me.
And I can't be found.

I want you to stay, and now they can't be found.

Motherless Child

Mother was there for me.
Now she's gone.
What do I do in a world where I am alone?
I feel like a *motherless child.*

I Love Me

As he said, I love you.
I couldn't help you, but you see.
I love me more, and we will never be.
He watched me in amazement as I boldly spoke.
Tears rolled down his eyes because my love for him was gone.
Dwindling on a road of unforgettable love, I know it will never be.
"I will miss you," He said.
I am only here for a moment to help thee to be free.
My love for me grows deeper and deeper so now I see my life as it should
be.
Will I ever see you again?
I could hardly say yes.
As he said, "Goodbye, I love you, see."
I said, "No, you don't love me,
I love me."

Will I Be True?

It's another day again, and I am here alone.
I am on the floor, wondering about true love.
Would it find me to be true?
When it comes, will I be right?
My doubts are few in between
as I sleep in my bed, clinging to the sheets of unforgettable dreams.
That once had died, and now I wonder, will I be right to love again, *will I be
true?*

I Maybe Me

He's gone, and my past is behind me.
And I maybe me.
He's not here.
I am not thinking about what he's done to discourage me.
I maybe me.
No more sleepless nights wondering if I will make it through.
I maybe me.
No more arguing and fighting about things that's just not right.
I maybe me.
If my past comes, you see,
I will let it go like a raindrop that disappears in the ground.
I maybe me.
If I wonder about what ifs
then I will wonder about the ifs in life that have gotten me this far.
I am on a journey of peace, you see.
I maybe me.

4
GLAZING GLORY

America Will Stand

America is me.
I have been excellent throughout the century.
I stand in a land strong and mighty.
That upholds our stamina and dignity.
As we sigh, not for what will stand.
We protect all our people in a free land.
That will rise to all occasions when fear is at hand.
To let our enemies know that we will eventually stand.
We have been through each battle.
One after another and they all will fall.
I am America, and *America will stand.*

A Glaze of God's Glory

Why wonder if I am conscious
when my soul is lost.
Just *a glaze of God's Glory*
will set me free from being lost.
Free from the war within me
that I can't see.
Lost in despair from the grievous wars
that has kept me hidden within me
that wars within my soul
of the burning that captures me.
Burn so severely that I could not see.
I fight for my dignity so that

the Glaze of God's Glory will lose me.
Loss from the demons
that kept me underneath the trenches of darkness.
Heaven's gates wait upon me beneath the closed doors.
I see *a glaze of God's Glory* that has delighted me.

Jesus Christ Day

Thus, this season is Jesus reason
for another day is *Jesus Christ day.*
To be joyful and jolly for what He's done.
Throughout the year
as we look to Him
for His love and unforgettable dreams of happiness with fun.
Supplied without a doubt
if we don't faint and give in to life's disparity of flight.
When we look to Him,
our mission will begin again
to start another day
that floats into a year.
That will enlighten and carry out our purpose for Him
to say that Jesus is the reason for this here season.
With the love and compassion on a day
He gave to His people
on *Jesus Christ day.*

I Am Me

I am loved to be lovable.
I am humble to be humble.
I am graced to be grateful.
I am a joy to be joyful.
I am happy to receive happiness.
I am peace to be peaceful.
I am hoping to be hopeful.
I am me.

God's Love for You

Why wonder about *God's love for you?*

He always got your back when you love Him back.
Things may seem like nothing is working at the present moment.
But hold onto the next moment while thinking positive and knowing for a
phase that God loves you and will come to those who love Him back.
Wait in the presence of the spirit for another love moment from God, and
things will change.
Keep spreading love.
That's what will turn your situation around and change an evil soul to
accept and love you for who you are because of *God's love for you.*

A Father's Courage

Who can wonder about your courage?
Who can question your faith?
No one knows, but the powerful force from above
that will award thee gratefully.
All my life, I've known you as a strong father who never complained.
It took lots of courage, but still, you didn't complain.
What do we know about a person's faith?
When we imagination little.
Only the strength that comes from thee
is so powerful that no one should complain.

Encouraging Words Today

Imagine encouraging words
standing there.
Hesitating about a choice,
but no one would encourage him.
I listen to his limited voice.
I spoke. "Don't be afraid to move where you wouldn't be limited."
Sparkle was in his eyes and with a big grin on his face, he said, "That's what
I needed to hear."
He dashed off joyfully with a new direction for his life
to say, "Thank you for those *encouraging words today."*

Dear Cousin

How long does a person suffer from sin?
It might sound strange to say as one will see, but
how long will a person suffer before he is set free?
I am the sister of the victim, who speaks the truth, you see, but how long
can a person suffer before he is set free?
My cousin was sentenced to life without parole for a crime he committed,
and now he has served 17 years in prison and asks to be free.
What does a person do when another person's life is in your hands?
Do I make a stand for what's right, believe in forgiveness, or be silent when
he deserves a second chance?
I speak not on behalf of wrong,
but in between on God's side, you see.
We sin before God, as some of us will do.
We ask for forgiveness of our sins; what does God do?
If we come before God with a sincere heart
to confess our sins (1 John 1:9), God is faithful to forgive and clean us from
sins and set us free.
Some people will wonder how you can speak on behalf of the crime
committed against your brother.
I feel that God chastens a person for so long,
and when it's time for that person to be set free, it's God who he must
answer to and not me.
People will hold judgment against a person for the rest of their life.
Is that the right thing to do when we all want to be free?
My brother meant a lot to me and gave me joy while he was present on this
earth.
He was the only one who would come running when I needed help.
Now I have no one to call upon for that help, you see.
But I still don't hold a grudge against my cousin, you see.
My brother was here for a short time giving his heart to everyone who could
see.
On the day he passed away, he came walking into my house as the heavenly
clouds hovered around his feet.
He went into the fridge and looked back at me to silently saying,
"I'll see you in heaven one day."
I was dumbfounded as he walked out the front door, not speaking a word to
me.
He is in heaven so I may speak.
I feel that my cousin went before God to set himself free.

And if he didn't, it's not my will to judge him, but to do what I feel is right, you see.
My brother had a good heart that he would help anyone who needed him.
Still, it was unfortunate what happened between my brother and my cousin, and I know if my brother could speak on another person behalf, he would say, "Let it be."
He now has a second chance for a life with the possibility of parole or a full pardon to be set free.
I feel he has suffered long enough in misery, you see. If any of my siblings were in this kind of predicament they would want a second chance to be free. I was inspired to write this by God and reach out to his father. What other people think is their opinion and not mine, you see.

Heavenly Clouds

He walked by me.
Into my home, he went.
Heavenly clouds hover around his feet.
He looked at me to smile for the last time.
I could not say.
He walked by me, silently looking to say,
"Goodbye for the last time, until I see you
again, with me walking in the *heavenly clouds* one day."

Guided Wisdom

Searching for light
out of the blue.
When the right words of wisdom
appeared to guide me through.
In a direction, I needed
that was spiritual
and true. To guide me into a place
of enlightenment and peace that had once exalted
me and carried me through.

God Can Fix It

My way looks hard.
I try to figure it out.
I will make it through tonight.
I put my trust in God,
and I watched Him see me through.
I know that *God can fix it*
because right now, I can make it through.

Hold onto Faith

Caught into a life of pain and misery.
How do I know how life is supposed to be?
But I know that I must not give up
on life's disparity.
I must faint not and must *hold onto faith*.

Brightness of Light

Brightness of light
shines.
Within my piercing soul
is the light not within me to see.
I hope to capture
the beauty of life that the light holds.
To shine like a jewel that is
held high upon a shelf.
Letting go of my beauty
that only I know about the *brightness of light* tonight.

Ethiopia

Woe to you land beyond the river sea.
Judgment will come upon the antichrist army.
Jehovah lifts and blows His trumpet.
Hear ye, hear ye as the angels will sing.
The night shall be as light as of the day.
And they will be destroyed while the morning breaks.

Ethiopia will submit to God,
and bring presents unto thee.
As our Holy Father rests for last time
because He has gotten the victory.

Double Portion

Sleep tight, little one,
and don't you peek
at what God Almighty is fixing to bring thee.
Double portion for your troubles
has come before God
to be released unto thee.

Eyes of the Beholder

The *eyes of the beholder* are great and sweet.
The power of the Almighty is for all to see.
With the hands of iron
and His rod is His defeat.
The *eyes of the beholder*
will engulf and capture me to see.

Flight of a Journey

Why do you wonder
about the flights of life?
God is the provider
that won't let you forget tonight.
He is what's right,
the great I Am.
Getting us through the tough times
to win the *flight of a journey* tonight.

This Day

Trying to hold on to life

as it is passing away.
Help from you, Lord,
in one moment, one hour, one day,
one week will make a year on *this day*.
I need to travel through a day
with a moment of your help, Lord.
You send your angels to engulf me,
to shadow me with your love as I pray.
All I need is one foot in front of the other one
as I walk to make it to another hour *this day* so
I may live to see my double portion
to help someone one day.
When my burdens were enormous,
I breathe a new breath of life
to get through this week today.
All I need is you, Lord,
to guide me through this perilous fight
for what's right.
What did I do to go through years
of a dreadful life, all my life?
Now I see why I was in this place.
Standing to stand more
as an excellent example for you,
God, when I can't fight.
You gave me the wits to fight so
I might receive my double portions
for all my years I lost tonight.

Pretending to Pray

It's best to obey and pray
as you seek God while He is there.
Before you get in distress, and He might not be there.
Pretending to pray
will only bring judgment on you someday.
It is best to be obedient and pray
because what if an opportunity comes your way?
Early in the morning
when you're supposed to pray.

Sins Flow Down

The flow of the rivers.
They go down.
The flow of the rain and snow from heaven
go down and never return.
The flow of our tears.
They go down.
The flow of the ocean's draft in the sea
goes down.
Our Holy Father forgives our sins.
They go down.
And never return as our *sins flow down.*

The Light Within

The light within us shines as bright
as the stars in the night.
The eternal light of love to
brings all a shiny delight.
Light of love gives freely to all
and to all who can imagine the gift of life to give.
Light of a clear day
that never wavers its strength
to neglect the ones who love the light for being light.
The light of the unknown shines brightly within us so
a person can see and gather the knowledge
to live by, be governed by, and to stand firm.
It's the light of the world that keeps burning bright.
It's the light of the world
that saves us from our terrible flight at night.
The light brings compassion
to all who gathers its strength
from God who loves *the light within* tonight.

Hidden Secrets of the Heart

The *hidden secret of the heart*
is a place to find God's heart.
Hidden beneath its path
is the plot of defeat.
The pain that the secret releases
is the flow of truth
that will enlighten you to be new.
The heart is the gateway
to generate the ideal of happiness.
Only you the beholder will magnify it
to release the *hidden secrets of the heart.*

Wow Is What I Am

Wow
is what I am.
I am the victory
to have all that I can.
A life of guilt and disguise, you see.
Victory is mine to engrave its image
in my soul where the deaths of hell engulf and behold.
Free at last, free at last from the devil's plot.
Now I am just me.
Wow is what I am.

Blessed Stream

Streams of blessings flow down.
Flow down upon me like a diversity frown,
frown beneath my soul that rises at night
to engulf me with this terrible flight.
To live and let life be so that I will be.
Be ready to say one day I have gotten the victory.
As this *blessed stream* flows beneath me.

Supernaturally Exalted

Supernaturally exalted is beyond a point of relief.
Test, trials, and obstacles I have overcome thee.
I see the horns of a ready writer.
Finally, ready to peak a sign of relief,
to be given the knowledge of time
that the whisper of wisdom triumphs and victory speak.

I'm Standing There

Is he standing there to forgive me in an empty world
that has forgotten me?
I hold to the stride that someone would think about me.
But there is no one there to forgive me.
My troubles are too hard to bear for me.
I look around, and nobody is there for me.
Trapped inside of me is a pain.
That won't let me become the person I claim.
Are you standing there?
I am standing right here.
Beside you walking you through
hoping that you would say, "Help me."
Because then you'll look on the side of you,
you'll see *I'm standing there* trying to help you.

Eagle Grounds

Think like an eagle
as you take charge of the enemy.
An eagle does not fight a snake on the ground, you see.
He picks it up and changes its ground to be deadly.
He takes the snake high in the air
where he has no power, no stamina,
and no balance to fight to be free.
He releases it back to the ground
to take control of the enemy.
Change your grounds like the eagle

and when you're in a tough fight to get the victory on *eagle grounds.*

God Has Something Just for Me

What does God have for me?
I can now see.
How did I make it this far?
Only by the grace of God
that guided me.
That only I could see.
God had something just for me.
There was no way to escape
what I've been.
He has something for me
and now I am true to know
that *God has something just for me.*
His plan.

Write On, Write On

Awaken once again with sleep nowhere in sight.
Do I pray, or do I be in peace through this night?
I see visions of things that might be.
I am hoping for the revelation of my dreams
that is there and wants to let me be.
Write, my daughter, write about what you will see.
I reveal to you your destiny.
The destiny of what's to come and it will be.
Just like I, the Father, says, "It will be."
Write on; write on until it flows like water.
Deep down from within, your spirit is where
the flow of birth begins.
It begins with a pen ready to breathe.
Breathe the breath of life as your source
within you begin.
Write my dear write of the wondrous light that shines
within you, for all to take flight.
The flight is the breath you breathe on this here night.
Flights that will begin as you
Write on; write on, yet another night.

Meant for Me

God, help me.
To help another on a day for me.
He removed my burden from me
so that I can help another, you see.
What to do when things are wrong?
Kneel to pray to say,
"Holy Father you can help me
so that I can be a blessing to another
on a day *meant for me* so that I can get through."

Mind of Paradise

Our mind controls thee.
Everything you hear and see.
Everything takes place in the mind,
and then it passes to the body to get results you see.
The results can be the outcome
of how long we last on this earth.
Mind over the body experience makes us strong.
We take control of our mind, and then your body will follow.
A free mind is a gift to have, even if you are weak.
You can think of yourself to have more.
You can talk to your mind
and make it do just what you want it to do.
Freely thinking can keep your mind at peace.
Teach your mind to feel loved,
and you won't have a problem
trying to find the *mind of paradise.*

Revelation of Talents

God gifts to you are talents without measure.
The rivers are flowing in your life.
Play it like you play a violin.

The rivers flow down upon you
like a waterfall with different colors
representing a rainbow.
The rivers divide into rivers.
Each river is a talent you play softly.
They all flow together
like a guitar with six strings.
You play each string differently.
Each talent is different in sound.
If you play them all together,
and they will all make one sound.
The strings can be whatever you want them to be.
Whatever talent that God gives you,
use it wisely so that you won't lose it.
Your talents will flow together
to make a sound like a beautiful flowing river
with many sounds.
Many rivers flow into it to make one river.
Walk daily with God's gifts and talents.
Your talents are gifts from God,
which is God's present to you.
Don't learn a gift; work to make it grow.
It comes naturally.
Learn how to play each string in your life
so all talents can work together to make one sound to God.
Talent gifts open doors into the pathway
for whom you are and your destiny.
Know your strength in each string,
in each river, and it will bring you God's happiness
as God reveals your *revelation of talents.*

Majestic Power

You once made me proud
as I could be.
To see me
just the way you made me to be.
Honored and clothed
in *majestic power.*
To glide into life

to find out
that all I needed was your
majestic power to get me through.

You Choose Me

Well, *you choose me, you choose me*
to be the person way back in destiny.
Before I came upon this earth
to move and float like a butterfly.
You choose me, and now if need be,
I am free to roam
on my ocean throne.
To float as I am meant to be,
now that you have chosen me.

Wondering Christian

A world of its own.
I am trying to fit in
to a world that is cold and alone.
Not fitting for a Christian,
if you know what I mean,
in a cold world where a *wondering
Christian* doesn't belong.

Assembly of Me

Forsake not yourself to assemble with me.
My foundation stirs up continuously
in the love of the Word of Christ, you see.
Let not your heart be troubled
because I hold the key to the book of remembrance.
Remembering those who feared and loved me
and hoping that none would be lost, but set free.
Through Jesus Christ's blood, each sin goes away.
You will live in the glory of God

to fulfill your mission and purpose in me
to have a good life in Christianity.
And that good life will set you free
to have a close relationship with me
in the fullest of time and happiness
when you can find peace of mind in the *assembly of me.*

Blessed Thoughts

My thoughts I have for you are blessed
to carry you through the drought
so that when your blessings come,
you will know that I did it for you without a doubt.

If Need Be, Then Let It Be

If need be,
then all I have is me
to fall in life
from my misery.
That engulfs my soul
until I have no room to breathe.
Maybe I'll just let the need be then let it be.

Wondering Soul

Why is your soul wondering?
When all you need is me
to get you through the life of the world's misery.
That comes so cruelly
that even a fool can see.
That maybe I'll pray
because life is a wandering prey.
To capture me as I linger into my destiny
with its awful fanes
as if my life is a rolling freight train.

Hopeless Despair

Yes, they say
that all I need is you
when I go through
hopeless despair.
In a world of pain
that has engulfed me
to be someone else
that I can't accept
who is in *hopeless despair.*

Illustrated by Me

How I made it to be
as the words were given to me.
Created and designed
and *illustrated by me.* That only I can see how the end will be.

Sound as a Rock

Yes, they say life is hard
when you're lost and not found.
A God who can only remove hardness
and make life sound.
Sound as a rock,
that's what God can do.
When you are in trouble
and can't see your way through.

Grandeur Power

Grandeur in power,
that's how God made me to be.
To be grandeur in power
with a clench of majesty.
Wondering on the hunt

looking for all
to conquer and never fall
as I enter the unknown power of it all.

Mighty Lion

I am a *mighty lion,*
gathering all as I crawl
to lure into my trap.
The weakness of them all.
To be mighty in my kingdom
That was given to me.
To sit and watch as I hunt,
so that biblical words will never fall.
I am the *mighty lion* that wears the crown.

Black and White Stripes

Black and white are my stripes,
given to me
without a doubt.
So that I would be different
from the others who see.
Only to have a mark
that will set me apart.
To be the chosen one
and the unforgettable one
that no one else could be.

New Dreams

The time of *new dreams* has come.
And winter is gone into the depth of the horizon.
Fall might bring me a sound of joy,
or it might be the spring
that will bring me *new dreams.*

Thank You, Holy Father

Thank you, Holy Father,
for all you done when I could not see me.
For without your help
I could not be me.
Thank you, Holy Father,
for your love and kindness
that keep me in love when
only I felt nothing to feel.
Thank you, Holy Father,
for not letting me fall
and stay in a dark place
that didn't recognize me.
Thank you, Holy Father,
for all that I can see
when I was blinded
and could not see.
My eyes opened so
that I could see the place for me.
Thank you, Holy Father,
for keeping me
from the dangerous pits of destruction
and devastation of what's intended for me.
You keep me through it all
just for me to see
that I am what I need to be.
Powerful and magnificent
in all before me
in a time when life was cruel and tried to entrap me.
Thank you for your Son Jesus
for all He has done,
for without His sacrifice,
where would we be in a careless world full of uncertainty?
And if I am not careful, it would entrap me
into a place where I used to be.

I'm a Queen

Miss Queen is my name that was
given by God.
He chooses me to walk tall
with phenomenal confidence
in a world that seems so small.
Knowing who I am
as I walk in the morning breeze
knowing without a doubt, I'm *a queen.*

Who Am I?

I am He.
And He is in me.
Cause I know whom I'm supposed to be.
That's why I know
He is with me.
Because I know who I am.
And that's me.

A Chance of Trust

Can I trust you in my venerability?
When I need someone to share my misery?
Can I trust you
to say okay
or will you turn my venerability into an awful prey?
What lurks at me
every chance it gets
to say you can trust me,
but really, you can hurt me.

Created and Designed Me to Be

I don't look like what I've been through,
because He is with me is more than them against me.
He *created and designed me to be* a
conqueror to them that hate,

who me?
The whole world's population will see
whom God has *created and designed me to be.*

Let Life Find You

Why be brief
when you have me?
I'm waiting for you to exalt me.
Why can't you be and *let life find you?*
In the world that you're in
winding and winding to find me.
What's not lost, but right before your eyes
is the gift of time.
I've given to you
to be all that you inspired to do.
Be thankful and not regretful of what lies ahead
to know that all you must do is breathe and *let life find you.*

One Word

Just *one word* from you
is all that I need to get through.
Encouraged and unforgettable will be all I need.
Day by day
and moment by moment
await me as I approach
a new life of dreams
that you gave me
once upon a time before anyone knew me.

Prophecy My Life

Prophecy my life
That's what I'll do.
I wonder on this earth
what seems true?

As life takes me into unfamiliar times
that I hope would leave.
I would regret and repent
of the things that the body controls and unwinds.
It unleashes the right prophecy in me to set my life at peace.

Aha

Aha
and wait for me
to tell you
what your life needs to be.
Not of uncertainty,
but life just what you need to be.

Finish Line

I was afraid to speak
then the Heavenly Father touched my lips to speak.
I walked into my destiny, unsure of what it would be,
then the joy of the Lord overshadowed me.
I laughed at the uncertainty.
The Holy Spirit overwhelmed me
to know what my purpose was in me.
Now I can finally see
as God ministered to a helpless soul
that was waiting to be free.
Deliverance came into the room
and overshadowed me.
Keep your eyes on the price,
and you will know where the *finish line* ends
as you cross the opposite sides.
It will deliver you from the hidden treasures inside of you.
Keep your eyes on the prize.
The reward is more significant
once you cross that *finish line.*

Mystery Unfolds

The devil flight on this journey
is hard to believe.
The critical thing it exposes to the soul make
me wonder; will it be brief as it unfolds?
Or will he bring a mystery?
Whatever it be,
I will know that God will be
there as the *mystery unfolds*
in the distance-time as my mystery is told.

God's Plot

I am wondering and wondering
about this here life.
Is it what I was supposed to be?
Should we carry on *God's plot* in this life?
Maybe what if it's not right
and go wrong?
What do I do when I can't sing a song?
Do I freeze up and just let it be?
Or do I wait on God to set me free?
Or maybe it's just how it's supposed to be.
God's plot reveals my life in me.

A Day of Wondering

All I need is you
to get through this day.
I am wondering if I would make it through.
Or would I be safe to say?
If I wonder too long, then what if I am alone?
Wondering in the forgotten
will bring hope to this home.

I say I am free
from the life you see.
I wonder if I am the only one
that knows that they can be free.

Hopes and Dreams

Why wonder on disparity
when life is good.
Hopes and dreams lie underneath my wings
to bring new life to unforgettable things.
Things of wondering
as life brings its foes.
Of the unforgettable drenches
that lies beneath the holes in our souls.

Uplifting Dreams

I hope for a new life
to bring me true destiny.
I approached life's crisis
when my life is in disbelief.
Wondering about tomorrow,
will it be correct for me?
Or will it be a hope of lost blues?
Waiting and hoping for the great things of God
to crush the underworld beneath my feet.
Uplifting dreams, I wonder, will it happen now
or will it be when I can't see?

Approached Destiny

Away with its destiny
as my soul approaches.
The new height is its being
of unforgettable things,
things of the unknown
that will leave the time behind.
Hoping for a new day

to breathe new life,
of it on that may have never been.
Approaching its destiny
to the beginning
and hoping for all to gather its wheat
of a replenishing harvest.
Life brings unforgettable things.
I do not know what this life will bring
as I *approached destiny.*

For They Need Your Help

Holy Father, help them,
for they need your help.
I lift the parents of the disabled,
for they need your help.
I lift the psychotics,
for they need your help.
I lift the suicidal people,
for they need your help.
I lift the homeless,
for they need your help.
I lift the restless in the soul and spirit,
for they need your help.
I lift the politicians,
for they need your help.
I lift the forgotten,
for they need your help.
I lift the sick and bedridden people,
for they need your help.
Holy Father, help them,
for they need your help.

The Goodness of God

I think about *the goodness of God.*
He brought me through.
I think about *the goodness of God.*

He shelters me to be safe in His arms to get through.
I think about *the goodness of God.*
In how He made away
out of my way.
I think about *the goodness of God.*
In how He made a
way for me to be fearless
to have faith in the *goodness of God.*

By You Through You

By you through you,
Holy Father, I dream again.
By you through you,
Holy Father, I have hope again.
By you through you,
Holy Father, I live again.
By you through you,
Holy Father, I am new again.

Purpose Life

I see life as a purpose
no matter how good or bad it might be.
It is controlling my selfishness.
Oh, how I refused to be sad
when God has so much for me.
It's easy to be bitter, mean, or mad
when all you see is bad.
Turn it into determination,
and change your life for the better
into a purposeful life that is not sad.

Soiled Hands

The soil in your hands
will calm the soul.
Where you will know of a place to find
that will be challenging to the mind.

To learn life skills
to have a peace of mind.

Setback of Opportunity

Worrying about what ifs in life
will only get you in a place of
unwarranted worries.
I should have done
a setback of opportunities
that will hold your life back
from a place of enlightening purpose
of how your life should be.

Well Done

Let me know
before I lose the battle with life
that has been a life I didn't want to know.
Now that I am here,
I might as well understand
that I must keep fighting.
If I am good and not evil
one day, I will hear God say,
"*Well done,* my good and faithful servant."

Obstacles in Sight

Waiting on a movement,
I wonder will I find another love movement
These obstacles are hard and weary to fight.
Sometimes it makes me lose
what's insight.

At Peace

I don't feel alone.
I feel at peace.
Loving the most important person
has kept me.
Jesus, I know
you hear me as I speak.
My life, my journey, my mind
is all *at peace.*

A Father's Love

Your arm wraps around
me like wings of warm feathers.
You, Holy Father, are everlasting,
Everlasting, and everlasting.
Why should we complain about
your power, might, and your love?
When your love is the Mighty of the Almighty?
A *father's love* that will endure
forever and forever in me.

5
UN-RISEN WORDS

Poem George Floyd
Blood Cried from the Ground for Justice

God is tired of sin.
When will justice win?
When will racism end
because of the color of our skin, black?
It was enslaved by the name given to us to be triggered by guilt that lingers
inside of us.
Why do we hurt so badly from the pain of those who engrave our soul with
doubt of who we are?
What we supposed to be?
Where have we come from?
Are we from the same planet of the people who affect our souls?
We are all from the same creator.
Only the light floats within us to be great of whom we are
To be greater than the cause of violence that is upon our necks.
Greater than murdering *George Floyd* to see him take his last breath while
he passed into another world,
Would we not know that the wrath of God would come for justice?
Death caught hold of his soul for eight minutes and forty-two seconds.
Grievous attacks on our destiny lie within us without a cause.
Do we fight for a sign of relief only to be taken for granted because of the
color of us, black?
When will our soul stop crying from the blood of the earth?
Have we lost enough death tolls?

When will we see that racism hurts all, not just black?
God ordained *George Floyd* on this earth for a time to change the world about racism.
The blood of *George Floyd* cried from the ground just as Abel blood cried from the ground in Genesis 4:10 to be heard by the Holy Father.
The blood of the resurrected saints will be uncovered.

Poem Breonna Taylor

Breonna Taylor eyes sparked and smile on her face moved us all.
To know the abhorrent reality of police brutality is apparently real and we are tired of it all.
We are angry and hurt; we can't shut it out at all.
She was happy to be alive, while police brutality abruptly ended it all.
A mother lost that is gone forever as the three un-uniformed men without a warrant with guns drown enters into her home without permission at all.
He shot five bullets and killed her soul, her spirit, her dreams, and her plans and her future all.
Two month after the execution of George Floyd, Breonna death was finally in the light of the wake of it all.
But in Breonna's death no one was charge at all.
In the wake of it all the beauties of Breonna personality shines to mimic it all.
Her partner was trying to protect her from it all.

Black and Police
About Innocent Black and Innocent Police

President, I think not what I see; Can you wonder anymore?
The pain of the world is in an uproar for all to see.
Democrats and Republicans, can you see what the world would be because the brutalities of men have come upon the hands of thee to change the world?

Pastors, you must take a stand in fasting and praying until *the black and police* brutality stops. Can you not see that the innocent lives need to be in our prayer each moment?

Senators and Congress why wait on a word hoping that the bloodshed would stop. Can you think to help to enlighten thee?

Wife and husbands, can you see the sight of your loved ones
as they go out to protect thee?

Mothers and fathers observing and wondering that their burden of the night would stop as they enter a grief-stricken period of total disbelief, uphold and uplift your burdened heart from thee.

The hatred has been heard all around the world.

Black and police, my heart is with thee as you are gun down by some without a care as if it's a plea.

War and rumors of war have come upon thee by the shocking brutality.

The nation is on edge, rallying, not knowing what will come of thee.

The shoots to the *black and police* officers as if they are alike.

Our hearts are warm with fear as we protest peacefully into the night.

You are ambushing *black and police* as if all are bad.

Beneath their hearts are innocent *black and police* fall.

The blood cries beneath the ground as we weep for the innocent lost soul in peace.

That somehow was shot by the ones who we look up to only to be fatally wounded by the hands of them for only a plea.

Mystery of Love

The secret of love is silent tears. The degrees that love flows are insignificant to time of measure. Its degrees enlightened by heightening of pleasure and time. Irrelevant time must not overlap when all you must do is keep the important and the significance of time pleasurable. Mountain of time awaits you in pleasure. The sea crease of time is engaging by all its matter that will bring new life to come. All matter needs love to capture the best moments. Breathe in the distance of time, and that time won't even matter, not even when the significant time will disappear in the atmosphere of love triangle when we seek our flesh to uphold the good in life. It's always falling because only the good must come from a stance of a love measure. Hallow be thy name of the goodness of our father that must breathe new life for the existence of time and pleasure. Matter must take place now that it took to make that matter exists. No, all the earth's atmosphere wonders about the unknown truths in life. The pleasure of time wants matter if you can't, and you must breathe the atmosphere of that time that matters the most. Insignificant time must always matter so the goods must flow through for the sequence of time as it lapses back into space matter in all issues of space, especially when time must stand still for existence to matter. The time of the aftermath of the stress must exalt all measures so time meets time again.

The Stranger Speaks

My head drops down while my eyes suddenly close.
My eyes arise in disbelief as the stranger before me speaks.
I am agape with fear as I look in disbelief.
A man that says you are the one suddenly speaks.
He looked at me as though I am here and will go nowhere.
Then, silently, I arise to speak.
Frightened and dumbfounded as I look upon him with grief and disbelief.
How did you get here?
Who are you?
I would have never chosen you.
Then *the stranger speaks.*
I am the one.
I've been here all along.
I am waiting to capture you as you are speaking in disbelief.
I gripped you when the stranger controlled your mind.
And I *the* stranger speaks.

Dark Peace

Darkness surrounds me.
But I am still at peace.
Just a little sleep is all I need.
Now that I know how to be at peace as I sit silently.
Dark peace I find to be pleasant within thee
as darkness surrounds me when I am at peace.

Unknown Journeys

Breathe new life as your journey takes you into the unknown.
Trials, tests, and obstacles may not be for thee.
But wait to see if you will breathe a sigh of relief
at the night and new things in life waiting on thee.

Mental Poison Vitamins

"What if" and "I should have done" are the devil's principal place of total disbelief.
That will take you into a weary state of total disbelief,
a dosage of *mental poison vitamins* that will be your grief.
Poison that will lure in the body and destroy your purpose and destiny. It will take you through an awful phase of life as you try to buy back old times trying to be relieved from the *mental poison vitamins* that will be your total defeat.

Unspoken Dreams

I only saw good until I faced you.
Alone and frightened in a world that has forgotten about me.
A heart full of sadness from what I used to have.
Unspoken dreams that made me rise from a place of despair to
only face a world alone and in hopeless despair.

I Have Nothing to Say

I have nothing to say so get out of my way
so that I can pray to be in peace today.
I have no poems to write and nothing to say today.
I was awakened from a dream
with nothing to say today.
If God has something for me to say,
then He would say.
I would write it down.
But *I have nothing to say.*

I am wondering what to do.
What God wants me to say.
I don't know so I hope that I'll be at peace today.
Maybe I should pray.
But what do I pray for when *I have nothing to say*?
So, I will probably pray so that my life would be safe.
In case I uniquely missed God today.

Sneak Peek

I saw a devil today as he drove in his car.
Head-on, he tried to kill us
as my dad swirled his car.
I peeked up to see
as I was in the back seat.
A man with blistering red eyes
with horns coming from thee.
Raced by from a place, I don't know where.
The dust caught the night air
as he roared passed me
into a place that wasn't for me.
I am not looking back to see.
As the devil drove by not to catch a *sneak peek*.

What Do I Do?

What do I do? What do I do to a life that has left me barren and unreal to be
true? Do I forget my past or let life be a reality?
Do I leave the devil and take back all that is mine?
I will take it back with a vengeance as I fight for what's divine.
I am never looking back at the past for what the demons have now lost.
What does a lady like me do?
To be faithful so *what do I do*?

Disparity as I Sleep

In the silence of the night, I can't sleep.
All I hear is my heartbeat within me.
Breathing and hoping for a peek of sleep.

As time lingers into the early morning dawn, I still can't sleep.
Maybe this morning, I can generally breathe because my mind is weak for a
new breath of fresh sleep. My eye lingers unto hopeless *disparity as I sleep*
to wonder when I will finally fall to sleep.

AM and PM

AM brings the morning light,
and PM brings the darkness of the night.
I am between the intervals that won't let me sleep from depravity.
If I sleep in the morning, then the darkness creeps.
Within my soul, that brings no peace as *AM and PM* creep upon me.

Silver Spoon

You once made me to be too low
when I could not see me.
In another life, I hoped to be
given a *silver spoon*
that would never be for me.
I'll never eat from a *silver spoon* that I'll never be able to hold.

Christmas Sting

Sleep, my Darlene, sleep into the *Christmas sting*.
Snap, crackle, and pop
go the weasel on this hot Christmas Day.
As it appears to be sunny and spring
when it's supposed to be a *Christmas sting*.

Endless Life

How long should he suffer from the hands of a person?
That ended his life before he became a man.
An *endless life* that passed away to soon
from the hands of his friend

that he thought ended too soon.

Released Thoughts

I have released my thoughts in my head
that I needed to release.
As I sleep in bed
to remember things, I thought was drenching me.
A life of dreams has caught up with me
as I release my thoughts into the sweet night.

Bittersweet I Sleep

A message of cold *bittersweet I sleep*
is coming to you as you sleep.
To wake you up at night
to wonder if what I see is real
or is it just *bittersweet I sleep?*

Happiness

Where can I find your *happiness?*
When I look, you are not there.
Maybe I need to prep my mind so it will be all that I have
or perhaps *happiness* is not lost
because I can find it in my sleep.
It will be possible for me to be happy if I change my mind so *happiness* will
come back to me as I sleep.

I Matter

I was willing
to lose it all
to gain it all
to win over me
because *I matter.*

Alone Journey

I'm on an *alone journey* on my own
that is complicated and alone.
I see another light
that is different in me.
A light to help me
jump out of reality.

Sleep Creeps

You will mess up my sleep,
as I try to shut my eyes
when *sleep creeps* up on me.
On the road, I choose not to go,
but it takes away
from whom I am
when *sleep creeps* up on me.

Me

All I have is *me*
to get *me* through
these tough times
where I can't flee.
Well it's only *me*,
and I'm sure
that's the way that it will be.

Passionate Thoughts

My *passionate thoughts* have left me for now,
so that I'll let writing be.
I'm tired now.
I can't think no more
because I've been writing for an hour in this mood, and my thought has
finally left me. For now, until it is again
as I want to write my *passionate thoughts* that will come freely.

Bubble Me Up

I drift dry
from the tears, I cry.
I'm in misery
and I hope this will soon leave me
so my bubble won't *bubble me up* and engulf me.

Drifting Sea

The land is drifting at a sea glance.
What a moment if I could recapture the glance.
As I drift away in the sand, lost in the wind
as the waves carry me into the ocean sea.
Never to return again
in this *drifting sea*.

Scripted Life

Well, what do you say to life journey?
That is an unforgettable script
that is written just for me.
Maybe it's for me to read
or perhaps it's for thee.
I'm not sure so I'll let my life script be.
Stuck lost in faith,
while waiting to be washed away
into the ocean's currency
never to be seen or heard
because maybe that's how I want it to be in this *scripted life*.

Unspoken Life

Why are you waiting for me in an *unspoken life?*
I want it to be.
I won't be caught
in a life that meant to be.
So that it won't wait for me to be in misery

because I have moved on
and now I only see the *unspoken life* is still waiting on me.

Bitter Life

Wait now,
what do you say about this *bitter life?*
Am I in doubt
about a painful life?
Only if I could see
that all this should be.
A life of accepting the good and evil,
which one would it be?

A Journey Life

The *journey of life*
brings misery and doubt.
Maybe this year, I'll bring me into what I need to be
or perhaps it will bring grief
into my life that I want to leave behind me.

The Past Me

Why wait on *the past me*?
The wind passes by.
Not holding onto
what brought me to a run.
Lingering on as I should be
and hoping for a life free of the *past me.*

Dreaded Soul

Why does life hurt so badly?
Life should be like the beautiful daisy grass.
But it withers away like the seagrass.
Must we say no to life?

Or should we say yes as we encounter the challenges
that we face when we are unaware of the *dreadful soul?* Like the breeze of
the switching air
blowing from God knows where.
Wait to what lies ahead
and it might be what you are feed
or it might lead you to the dead
as your *dreaded soul* waits what's ahead.

Blue Life

What about life?
When I've been true?
I was hoping for another insight to find you.
I do not know what the future would do.
Maybe my soul needs love the most
when I can't see it when I feel that sometimes
all I see is a *blue life* that will never be true.

Unreasonable I See

Hey, what can I say about
this here thing?
That is clinching on me
with a clinch that can't be found.
When I look for it,
it disappears in the sky.
Waiting and exhaling for another breath to be near me
as my journey approaches me for the *unreasonable I see.*

Dong

Dong, why has it been so long,
since I heard a word from you?
All I've been doing is trying to seek you.
I'm seeking your knowledge
and your wisdom so
I can win this fight that I fight daily
in a temperance mood that is swift and cruel.

Swish Wash

Swish wash, swish wash,
and just let it be.
Running back and forth in life
won't set no one free.

Unnamed Return

Well, time for me to go.
Not sure when I'll return.
It might be this summer
or perhaps this fall.
If it is winter,
then I know that I'll
see that I will be the person
unnamed in my return, I'll be.

Yes, Indeed

Yes, indeed
is the best answer to give
when your soul is in doubt
and you don't know
where to begin.

Double Lines

Suddenly life approaches me,
and I don't know what to think.
I might wander and become
all that life is said to be.
Maybe I'll take an approach
and hope that I'll make it through
the journey of the *double lines*
that is awaiting me.

Precious Memories

In a distance memory,
I see you.
I think of how you love us to be.
We should treasure each moment
as if it's our last and not hold back on the distance of time.
Memories are precious.
I think about how it used to be.
I wonder about the love we shared,
and then it was gone
never to be found again.
Hold on to the *precious memories*
of how good things used to be.
Without those memories, we could not see
how you love us to be.
Hold on to the memories.
Don't let them leave.
Hold onto the memories.
They are all we have.
If we didn't have the memories,
then we would not know how our past would be.
Hold onto the memories.
The memories will help set you free
to the life we once had
with the newness of God on our way to our new journey.

Clouds

When I grew up as a child,
I wonder about life.
Would I make it through with faith?
Or would I be drowned in disbelief?
As I looked around,
I could see we were suffering.
I wonder if they ever thought about it
or maybe it was in their dreams?
I see this life isn't what it's supposed to be.

I wonder would someone help me
so that I would be free?
Would I have to encourage myself
with my prophecy?
As I looked up to the *clouds*
to say that one day I'll be free and
have the life I wanted it to be.
Only if I could see
and only if I could hear
someone say, "I love you" and "I hope you great success
and you'll get all that you deserve."
Those words would be encouraging to get me through that moment.
As I looked up into the *clouds* for the last time to say *clouds* be with me
today.

Hurting Mind

My mind is hurting.
What do I do?
Is it an over camp of how I need to be true?
What if it lingers in a place I need not be?
Do I pull it out?
Do I pull through?
To get through this day
before it leaves me.
Until the next time, it will let anger be.
To write and write about the pain it holds.
A mind is a terrible thing to waste
when it's the behold
of the world's
things hidden in the soul.

Challenged Life

All I can do is think why.
Why are my words lingering?
What will take me into another world for its gain?

Do I be true to something that will hurt me?
Do I be wise
and not fall into the traps of life?
Sometimes life can be challenging.
Do we challenge it or let it be?
Maybe we need to wait on a word from thee
to show us where in this life we need to be.

Free at Last

Free at last, free at last
from this journey of pain.
All that I can see and do
is true.
Life threw me a wrench.
But I didn't get drenched.
In the downfall of the unfortunate
that sometimes loses all
to be whom they were to be.

Dream On, Dream On

Dream on, dream on,
and don't let disparity take your joy.
Life lessons are supposed to bring you a reward of joy.
At the end of its pain
will be your gain.
The newness toolbar you are supposed to be.
Don't complain about life
when it does what it's supposed to do.
If you stay right then you will know what you're supposed to do.

Wondering Life

Why wonder about life
when its approach is sometimes grief
that can be used strong
to be set free.
Life you see it as
what can it be?

Maybe unforgettable
or maybe just a dream
to show you just how you are supposed to be.

Ridden Beyond Belief

Why wait on me
when I don't wait on you.
Not in this life because I must escape *ridden beyond belief.*
You have trodden on me,
ridden beyond belief.
Will this be your last time?
I can see you were not here.
Not with me, not for me;
therefore, goodbye
for the last time
and I hope I don't see you again.
All I can remember is how bad you treated me.
Goodbye and I never want to see you again.
I found someone else to help me.
His name is God, and His son is Jesus, you see.
The other part of Him is the Holy Spirit that takes me on the journey to be
me.

Floating Raft

Why wonder about me
when I have God, you see.
All I need is a Word from thee
to make me keen to handle the life that is me.
So that you see,
all I need is God because I know that he is there for me.
To help His people on the journey they take
when life throws them a raft.
Will they sink or be in the *floating raft?*
Or will they just let life pass?
Waiting and exalting Jesus
when they don't know whom He be.

Disguise Fly

Wondering soul,
where are you?
I looked and looked and looked,
but I can't find your woes.
Maybe you are a set of disbelief,
or perhaps you are what I need to be.
O death,
I seek, sometimes, when my soul is lost.
Wondering into this life,
but only I can see
your plots of disguise waiting to catch the *disguise fly*.
As it lingers by hoping to flee
to the tree of life, you see.

My Last Breath

Desperate, I hope for this thing to be.
As life approaches me
with her agony.
Trying to take *my last breath* I have,
but I won't let it go because
it's all that I have, you see.

Road to Despair

Why be trodden
in a world of despair
when hopeless dreams are
on the *road to despair?*
Disparity, they call her by name
even when she breathes
relief from her growing pain
that won't let her be.
Free at last, free at last
she hopes to be
as she waits patiently

for a sign of relief on the *road to despair.*

Underneath the Tree

Why wait
for me when my hope is lost.
Lost so that now I can't see
if love follow me
then it would be brief.
To let it flow backward *underneath the tree.*
The tree of the unforgotten
that won't let my soul be.
But I can breathe,
if I breathe a sigh of relief
to know that I want to be heard
to breathe a good sigh of relief *underneath the tree.*

A Sinner's Soul

A sinner's soul
is lost to the behold.
Unforgettable as it reaches the breach.
Lost in time,
but never forsaken to be.
How destiny made it to be
never forgotten
to be its purpose and destination.
Waiting to exhale
as the wind blows its breath of awakening
so the sinner's soul will never be lost to be.

Sneeze Breeze Delight

Beneath the peak of my memories laid a trodden field of air that breathes
life into despair.
Why are thee trodden down when only you can see so many frowns?

Who lies beneath the stars under the light where the midst of a breeze
disappears into the twilight night?
Oh night, oh night, why have you trodden on my heart
to leave compassionate marks so that it won't depart into the *sneeze breeze
delight* tonight.

He's Been Away

I needed to hear him say that
it will be okay,
but *he's been away,*
and I can't say because *he's been away*
so long, and our love went away.

Silent Conversation

A glee of a happy relief
when I looked up into her eyes.
I once encouraged her to be all that she could be
in a conversation, we shared only between her and me.
Walking toward her in uncertainty
is the girl I encourage to be
on this day. She had no way home.
With happiness in her eyes to see me
as I encourage her
to be in college as she looked at me.
Stay encouraged and keep up the good work
as life takes you on a journey.
Because my joy and inspiration
come from thee,
whom I have helped to be whom you need to be.

Good Side in Me

You only saw the *good side in me,*
while I hid the pain in me.
Waiting for the right moment to release the grief in me
as I am hoping one day that the right side in me

will be true to myself and you.

Funny Life

Life is funny to me
how everything is.
That's waiting on me
as a sprint of a glee.
Changing the footsteps to move backward
and hoping to look forward.
Oh, life is funny to me.

6
DRIFTED WINDS

Hanging from a Tree

When I was young,
trying to sleep.
People asked me,
why do you sleep
as thou you're *hanging from a tree?*
Why do you move and move as though something is running behind thee?
I could never sleep in a bed, you see.
I never laid my head on a pillow
or sleep silently.
I slept as if I was *hanging from a tree.*
Legs and arms dangling out of the bed
with my head only in the bed
as if I was tied up swinging from a tree.
Sometimes I would be caught by mother
before I fall to the floor.
Never asking why,
just put me back in bed, you see.
Only to be pushed out of bed
until I am back *hanging from a tree.*

Twisted Mind Set Free

Two weeks have gone.
Satan got me wondering if I made the right choice to let it be.
Maybe if he would call and I hear his voice,
then I'll know he is not for me.
I made the right choice to let him go.
I can't help to think that I am lonely now,
and if he were here, maybe I wouldn't be,
but I would be in misery, you see.
Evil tries to come over me as I let go.
My mind needs someone who can lead and set me free.
Maybe it's the pastor I once called a stranger to help me.
I called him to say thank you for listening and helping and praying for me
when I was so weak and needed someone, you see.
I'll ask him to pray for me
so that I will remain steadfast in this unknown journey that tests and teach
me as my twisted mind flee.
Pray for me, man of God
so God will keep and protect me from the devil's plot while he tries to take
away my peace.
He prayed for me while I was so weak.
Then suddenly, I felt the power of God come upon me.
"Daughter, don't you weep. Be strong and courageous in this very moment
because the wiles of the devil won't let you sleep."
God renewed my mind so that I could be happy and go my way.
The Glory goes to God to allow the pastor to speak.
Bless you, pastor, as I speak.
I will call you back soon one day as he said,
"That's why I am here to help those who may stray away while needy
comfort to start another day."

Finally Set Free

I used to feel shutdown and never speak, you see.
I was trapped inside of me and couldn't break free.
Every day I am changing for the better,
and I thank God for that.
I can't believe that finally something that has helped me from hiding so
long.

It has been lingering for so long.
A new good life.
I am so glad I broke free from the garbage that came with pain.
I've come this far to be *finally set free* of my tears and misery.

My Past Is Gone

My past is gone, and I am here all alone.
It's not with me anymore.
I am living in the present, and that what it will be.
I'm looking into the future for a new present that will soon be true.
I'm looking at a new time, a new adventure that awaits me.

Past, You Must Go

That was my past.
And you must go now.
Past, you are not welcome
in my present or my future.
Past, you must go.

Since I Meet You

The one I love is
away in the cool breeze in the timid night.
Since I meet you, I've lost my mind and drifted out of time.
Darkness creeps in and surrounds me.
And the sun never shines on my aching body you left behind me.
Since I meet you, the wind chills my spine.
And the rain falls on me all the time.
Since I meet you, your venomous words are there.
Your voice terrifies me.
Your fist frightens me.
As you touch my lifeless body on a day
that I've finally learned how to live without you.

Weary Soul

Weariness in the soul
is a life of unwanted defeat
that can be broken by the power
of expounding relief.
That can be complicated in life
if you allow it to be your defeat.

Eyes of Misery

Eyes of misery
are the heart of the devil's defeat.
For grief in a dying soul
will be your defeat.

Trodden Despair

All go, you got to go.
Go away from here.
I smother myself in grief and despair
on the lonely road of misery.
I've have trodden down my soul.
Wait, until I say go.
Go from here now
because it's too late
because my life is in *trodden despair.*

Devil's Defeat

Hate on me if you dare because I don't care.
I got my victory when you have grieved despair.
I've gone on this journey alone.
I have gotten the victory of the *devil's defeat,* you see.

I Trust Me and Not You

You took my innocence as if I gave it away.

As if I said, 'Take it."
It's your fault for what he's done, they say.
Who cares?
They say that you let it happen to you
as he deceived you with his words, trust
me.
But no, in my mind,
I trust me and not you.

Whisper Surprise

The voice of a whisper cries and uplifts the sky when your heart is at its
biggest *whisper surprise.*

Forgotten

All I need is for me to be me.
Life has brought me pain and misery.
Why do you not want me when all I tried to do is teach you responsibility?
The world is not perfect for its deceit and despair.
All I wanted was the best for you,
even if it brought me despair.
It was my responsibility to raise you, even if I lost my way.
Hopes of the dreams I could not see that became distant memories.
I will recapture it one day, and all my pain will be lost.
Forgiven and cast away from me, but never *forgotten.*

Me Be Me

Once lost in the face of misery.
Yeah, it's me.
When I wake up this morning, I see me.
I saw my face as bare as it could be.
Yeah, that's the face I like to see.
The beauty of me now is so beautiful to see.
That the face I like to see is me.
Thank you, Holy Father, for letting *me be me.*

Redeemed and Set Free

This pain inside of me.
I want to be *redeemed and set free.*
God, I want to be redeemed.
I want you to set me free.
It won't let me go.
It won't let me be.
I don't want to go back.
God, please redeem me and set me free.

Drywalls Victory

Hold up, wait a minute, you.
Why do you want to treat me like a fool?
I am the queen, and you may be my king.
I keep you within these drywalls to get the victory.
To encourage the pain that might be within me.
Let go of me.
I have gotten the *drywalls victory.*

Bare Feet and Pregnant

Bare feet and pregnant
I once believed I might be.
You once said,
"That's what I will make you to be.
Lost in disparity,
hopeless and numb to life."
I bought it, but it wasn't filled with fun.
I must go away somehow
from a life I thought it would always be
a life given as I am *bare feet and pregnant,* and it will never be.

Dream On

I must *dream on, dream on,* my dear.
I must set the stage.
Life of uncertainty

for me.
Shame of disparity, I sought it to be
only in my dreams
will I be set free to *dream on?*

Unconscious Worry

Well, why worry when it brings grief?
That will lure into the bones of thee.
To make you unconscious
of what it's about to do to thee.

Worry Swell

The pain goes deeper
than what one can see
as it lures into your body to defeat thee.
Oh, how it will leave thee.
Unconscious in the mind
and the body as well
that only you will tell
when that senseless *worry swells.*

Happy Glee

Why can't I be happy as a glee?
The way I used to be.
When I try so hard,
it only fails me.
I'm wasting time that only I can see.
As they look upon me with amazement
and with a sign of happiness with a *happy glee.*

Silent Voice

The *silent voice* speaks
at a time I don't want it to be.
I am ashamed to let it come forth
and make me speak.

Hidden Me

Wonder upon my past,
and you will find the *hidden me*
inside of a person that is not me.
A person that I've tried so hard to change
into whom was I to be?

Disappointed Hope

You *disappointed me*
when I drive so far to meet you.
I was hoping that you would be the one to help me
and be whom God made me to be.
Maybe it's not the time for me
or perhaps me and not you.
Will I ever get a chance so
my hard work will pave the road for me?

7
MISSISSIPPI

Mississippi Grounds

Mississippi is my name.
I represent it in the gain
of the grassroots within my soul.
Popular for the lyrics sound it holds.
Ring within my soul, Mississippi.
Beneath the ground, Howlin' Wolf howls
at the pleasure of the sound
within the *Mississippi grounds.*
That's true to the heart of the music.
It rings in the earth's atmosphere, the melody of southern blues with B. B.
King mystery blues.
It is moving into the streams
with an unforgettable rhythm sound
that flows in all seasons.
Bringing its flow of charisma
as it lifts the soul of the unforgettable.

My Mississippi Music

Will we ever get rid of the shame?
Of the blood that my ancestors shielded in their faith of blood,

they claimed.
The shame of bigotry, the degradation of slavery,
racial and gender oppression that all dealt with pain.
That caused our minds to entangle in our identity
of whom we are and whom we must be.
That has marked our state to make people wonder to see.
Will Mississippi ever be set free of them all who fought to be open and
liberated from a cause.
They are trapped and engulfed when they could not see.
When all my people wanted was a change
for life for you and me.
We are standing strong now to be like the beauty we are
a flower that blossomed into a beautiful Magnolia State.
We try so hard to make Mississippi better because
we are the birthplace of America's music
that makes everything better.
The melodic sounds of the southern music
flows into all nations.
They dance and will never forget *my Mississippi music.*

My Mississippi

True to the heart of the music
as it rings in the earth's atmosphere.
The melody blues moving
into the movement with an unforgettable rhythm and blues.
Bringing the flow of love
as it lifts the soul of the people.
As it's dashing by, they will never forget
My Mississippi.

Mississippi Sing On

As we clap for joy at the sound of the Mississippi music
that will be our forever our joy.
It rings in the hearts of all who hold to its destiny.
We will never let the Mississippi music lose its purpose.
Never to be forgotten as *Mississippi sings on.*

Mississippi River's Path

Mississippi River's path flows beneath the wondrous holes
as it branches into a mystery scene of foes.
It brings life to the wondering creatures it holds.
Breathe a fresh ground of a gift of life to all in its path.
Flowing downstream in the swift drift
on its purpose to take the oath of the water
as the creatures swim beneath to the destination
that no one knows what life will bring in the wondrous path it holds.

Mississippi Blues

B. B. King the music of a king
in his strings
that touched all hearts with the sound of his guitar strings.
Its legacy will not be lost as it finds
even the true spirit in mind.
Bringing his music to life
as he finds the rhythm rhymes.
In the king of Mississippi songs
as he sings the *Mississippi blues* on his string.

Howlin' Wolf Ground

Beneath the ground,
his music flow through with a mysterious sound.
He became the man who let his guitar strings sound into the night.
Howlin' Wolf will never lose its steady ground at night.

March On, My Brother, My Friend, My Sister, My People

March on, march on, my people so we will influence the world so one day
we will all be set free from the struggles that we continue to fight.

March, my friends so we will obtain victory in the eyes of God who has
been there for thee. The eyes of the wise and in the eyes of the babes
so that one can see we will be free. That's a promise to all who hope in this
peace. We will be free to being whom we are to be of this world who came
knowing its curves.

March on, my brother, and to those who have lost the respect.
If men could have written about the imperfections,
would they seem so far?
To him, that has come this far not to give up his life for the gem,
but to wait for the final prize to finish the race with God's grace.

March, my sister, in the character, greatness, and of superior love of those
who accept you.
Capture yourself so the queen that you are will be set free.

Therefore, march on, my brother.
March on, my friends,
March on, my sister,
March on, my people,

Rhythm Cool Blues

Rhythm and blues are cool;
out goes laughter of midtown blues.
Which way it goes
dare to see.
If I can feel it
when they sing.
The feeling that comes with it
is healing to my soul
Mississippi mystery *rhythm cool blues.*

B. B. King String

B. B. King is the music of a king
that touched all hearts
with the sound of his guitar strings.
Never will be lost
of the legacy it finds

even the right spirit in mind.
Bringing his music to life
as they see the rhythm rhymes.
The king of Mississippi
sings the blues on his string.

Magnolia Tree

My beautiful *Magnolia tree* shines so widely.
As it spread its beauty that only is given with its sweet smell.
Beautiful as it stands to be Mississippi's strand.
To have a name given to thee
that all eyes will see.

Mississippi

Is
Southern
Scenery of
Interchangeable
Sound of rhythm and blues that
Smoother
In
Peace and
Perfect
In provision for what to come

In Mississippi

I wonder would I ever see him again.
Only to realize I had awakened from a bad dream again.
Maybe, he's just not coming back again.
Would I get lost in a world of sin, while hoping that he would find me
again? I wonder would I ever see him, until one day
we said, "Let's be best friends."
After all these years, he found me again *in Mississippi,*
where we first began.

Title: Despair

Visual Artist Linda Kay Chandler